Zoom in on
RAIL NETWORKS

Hannah Isbell

Enslow Publishing
101 W. 23rd Street
Suite 240
New York, NY 10011
USA

enslow.com

WORDS TO KNOW

cargo—Goods carried on a train, ship, or plane.

depot—A train station.

engineer—A person who designs and builds structures like railroads.

friction—The rubbing of one thing against another.

levitate—To raise.

locomotive—The powered car that pulls a train.

mass transit—A system of transportation for a large number of people. It usually include buses and trains.

parallel—Side by side, keeping the same distance in between.

rails—The steel bars on which trains run.

rail sleepers—The bars that connect two rails on a railroad track.

railway—Railroad tracks.

switch—The part of the railway system that helps a train move from one track to another.

trolley—A carriage that rides on tracks.

CONTENTS

Words to Know 2

1   Riding the Rails 5

2   The Age of Steam 9

3   Electrified! 16

4   The Future of Rail 19

Activity 22

Learn More 24

Index 24

Today's trains can go farther and faster than ever before.

Riding the Rails

Have you ever taken a train ride across a long distance? You probably had an interesting view of cities and countryside as the train zipped along. But imagine going so fast everything is just a blur! Today's high-speed trains carry passengers at speeds of up to 160 miles per hour (257 kilometers). They can make trips in a few hours that would take days by car, and engineers think that someday they could go even faster. Riding the rails has come a long way!

Before Steam

When you think of the history of railways, you might picture a steam locomotive, with loud whistles and puffing smoke. But long before the steam-powered train was invented, people used rails to help move things from place to place. Rails are a pair of steel bars laid parallel to each other on the ground to make a track. They are connected by a series of rail sleepers, beams or bars that keep the rails an equal distance from each other.

Early rails were used for carts pulled by people or animals. They were used for hundreds of years. Then people began linking the carts together to make trains, so that they could haul more in a single trip.

Without rails, trains would have nowhere to go!

A Hilly Railway

One of the oldest railways still running is at the Hohensalzburg Castle in Austria. It is a funicular railway. It uses ropes or cables to haul cars up and down steep hills. The castle's railway has been in use for more than five hundred years!

Fun on Rails

Roller coasters use the same idea as funicular railways to pull cars up the first steep incline. Instead of a rope, roller coaster cars are pulled by a cable belt until they reach the top. Then they are released to speed down the tracks!

The Age of Steam

Before steam trains, people rode the rails in horse-drawn trollies. But then a new invention changed rail travel.

In 1712, a British inventor named Thomas Newcomen developed the first steam engine. A steam engine uses heat from water boiled by burning wood or coal to make power. Newcomen's engine was used for pumping water in a mine, but engineers knew that with the right design it could work to power trains.

People ride in a horse-drawn trolley on rails.

Do the Locomotion

It took a long time and many engineers to make a steam engine that could move a train. Each inventor improved on the ideas of the last. Finally, in 1825, the first public steam railway was opened in England. It was designed by George Stephenson for the Stockton and Darlington

Railway and it was called the *Locomotion*. Stephenson's steam engines were a huge success. In a few short years, his company was building railways all over Europe and America.

Shaping History

Trains changed transportation across the world. They also changed people's lives in some unexpected ways! In America, trains were a large part of the movement to the West.

A Horse's Work

The power of an engine is measured in units called horsepower. This term came from the number of horses it would take to do the same work of the single engine.

An early steam locomotive

They allowed the country to grow faster than would have been possible before.

As railways grew, and more and more trains ran on the tracks, people had to work out ways to organize them. Rail networks linked cities and towns together. Stations (also called depots) were built where the trains would stop to let people board or to load and unload cargo. Passenger trains carried people from city to city, while freight trains transported goods.

Before trains, each city and town kept its own time, but to keep trains running on schedule that had to change. Everyone's clocks had to be set at the same time!

A steam train makes its way through the Sierra Nevada mountain range in 1875.

Busy Tracks

Train tracks crossed each other, like roads going in different directions. Signal systems had to be created. They allow a train's conductor to know when it is safe to stop and go. They also warn people who might want to walk or drive across the tracks that a train is coming.

Switches allow trains to move to a different set of tracks. They work by moving a small portion of the rails in order to guide the train in a different direction.

A junction is a place where two or more railway tracks come together.

Electrified!

Big cities like London, New York City, and Paris began building trains for mass transit. City streets were already crowded with people, carts, and carriages, so engineers took the trains above and below the ground. Elevated trains and underground trains, or subways, began opening at the start of the twentieth century.

The steam trains gave off thick black smoke that polluted the air. This was especially bad in big cities where there were

Super Subway

The New York City subway opened in 1904 and is one of the oldest mass transit systems in the world. It runs twenty-four hours a day, every day, and its trains travel underground, at street level, and elevated above the streets.

The elevated train system in Chicago is called the "L."

many trains. To help solve this problem, people turned to electricity.

The first electric-powered rail travel was invented in the 1880s. Electric wires were run above carriers called tramcars. For trains, a third, electrified rail was added along the ground.

Today trains are mostly powered by electricity or gasoline.

The Future of Rail

In 1964 the first high-speed rail lines opened in Japan. The trains are known as bullet trains. They travel at speeds over 155 miles per hour (250 km) and up to 200 miles per hour (322 km), but engineers believe it is possible to go even faster.

A bullet train in Japan

The Maglev

In the early 2000s, a new kind of train began operating in Shanghai, China. This train has no wheels and doesn't even touch its tracks! It is a Maglev train.

The name Maglev comes from "magnetic levitation." A Maglev train uses the energy of magnets to levitate trains, holding them up over the tracks. The magnet also pushes the train. Maglevs are the fastest trains in the world, in part because there is no friction from wheels to slow them down.

The Power of Magnets

Although magnetically powered trains are a new invention, scientists and engineers have been using magnets to levitate for over a hundred years!

A Maglev train runs through a vacuum tunnel.

The only thing that slows a Maglev train is wind resistance. This is the force you feel pushing against you when you move very fast (for example, when you put your hand out the window of a moving car). Engineers imagine a future system of Maglev rails inside tubes. Such trains could travel at thousands of miles per hour!

ACTIVITY
BUILD YOUR OWN TRACKS

You will need:

- popsicle sticks
- glue
- ruler
- toy train or car with moving wheels
- pencil and paper

Step 1: Prepare to Build

Rails keep trains on tracks. When you build your own rails, they must be the right size! Use a ruler to measure the distance between the right and left wheels on the toy train or car you want to drive on your tracks. When you measure, be sure to measure from the outside edge of one wheel to the outside edge of the other!

(Helpful hint: Place your model train or car on a piece of paper and make a mark with your pencil at the outside edge of each wheel. Then use a ruler to measure the distance.)

Step 2: Sleepers and Rails

To start building you will need seven popsicle sticks: two for rails, and five for sleepers. First, use your ruler to mark where you will attach the rails to the sleepers. Make two marks on each sleeper that are the same distance apart as you measured the wheels of your train or car.

Step 3: Lay the Rails

To make your first set of tracks, lay your sleepers out side by side about ¼ inch from each other. Then, put a drop of glue over each mark on the sleepers. Place the two popsicle sticks that will be rails along the tracks and let them dry.

Step 4: Test It!

After your first set of tracks are dry, test them by setting your car or train on them and rolling it. If you measured correctly, the wheels should be able to move while staying between the tracks.

Step 5: Ride the Rails

Build more sets of tracks and lay them on the table or floor to create one long track. Try out different turns and shapes for your tracks!

LEARN MORE

Books

Balkwil, Richard. *The Best Book of Trains*. New York: Kingfisher, 2008.

Cooper, Elisha. *Train.* London: Orchard Books, 2013.

Floca, Brian. *Locomotive*. New York: Atheneum/ Richard Jackson Books, 2013.

Websites

All About Trains
easyscienceforkids.com/all-about-trains/
Read interesting facts about trains.

History of Trains
www.dkfindout.com/uk/transport/history-trains/
Learn about all different kinds of trains and how they have changed.

INDEX

electric-powered rail, 18

funicular railway, 8

high-speed trains, 5, 19

horse-drawn trollies, 9

horsepower, 11

Maglev train, 20–21

mass transit, 16

Newcomen, Thomas, 9

signal systems, 15

steam engine, 9, 10

steam locomotive, 6, 10–11

Stephenson, George, 10–11

Published in 2018 by Enslow Publishing, LLC.
101 W. 23rd Street, Suite 240, New York, NY 10011

Copyright © 2018 by Enslow Publishing, LLC.
All rights reserved.

No part of this book may be reproduced by any means without the written permission of the publisher.

Library of Congress Cataloging-in-Publication Data
Names: Isbell, Hannah, author.
Title: Zoom in on rail networks / Hannah Isbell.
Description: New York : Enslow Publishing, 2018. | Series: Zoom in on engineering | Includes bibliographical references and index. | Audience: Grade K-3.
Identifiers: LCCN 2017003089| ISBN 9780766087095 (library-bound) | ISBN 9780766088412 (pbk.) | ISBN 9780766088351 (6-pack)
Subjects: LCSH: Railroads—Juvenile literature. | Railroad engineering—Juvenile literature. | Railroad trains—Juvenile literature.
Classification: LCC TF148 .I83 2018 | DDC 625.1—dc23
LC record available at https://lccn.loc.gov/2017003089

Printed in the United States of America

To Our Readers: We have done our best to make sure all website addresses in this book were active and appropriate when we went to press. However, the author and the publisher have no control over and assume no liability for the material available on those websites or on any websites they may link to. Any comments or suggestions can be sent by email to customerservice@enslow.com.

Photo Credits: Cover, p. 1 (inset) Leonid Andronov/Shutterstock.com; Cover, p. 1 (background) szefei/Shutterstock.com; pp. 2, 3, 5, 9, 16, 19, 22, 23 Elegant Solution/ Shutterstock.com; p. 4 He Shi/Moment/Getty Images; p. 7 Kevin_Hsieh/Shutterstock.com; p. 8 Joy Fera/Shutterstock.com; p. 10 Amoret Tanner/Alamy Stock Photo; p. 12 Lambert/Archive Photos/Getty Images; p. 14 Hulton Archive/Getty Images; p. 15 AleksSafronov/Shutterstock.com; p. 17 pio3/Shutterstock.com; p. 18 Tupungato/ Shutterstock.com; p. 19 Steve Allen/The Image Bank/Getty Images; p. 21 andrey_l/ Shutterstock.com; graphic elements (red rails) RFVector/Shutterstock.com.